*An Appeal To
Heaven*

Other Books By Dutch Sheets

An Appeal To Heaven

Dutch Sheets

Unless otherwise indicated, Scripture quotations are from the New American Standard Bible®, copyright © 1960, 1962, 1963, 1968, 1971, 1972, 1973, 1975, 1977, 1995, by The Lockman Foundation. Used by permission.

Published by Dutch Sheets Ministries
P.O. Box 764898
Dallas, Texas 75376
www.DutchSheets.org

Printed in the United States of America

ISBN-13: 978-1511540070
Title ID: 5407574

Cover design by Breanna Schweiger

Dutch Sheets
MINISTRIES

CONTENTS

INTRODUCTION

The Message

At the end of 2013, I realized I was ending a 13-year spiritual journey. It started during a prayer and ended with a flag. An old and forgotten flag; forgotten by everyone, it seems, except God. He had evidently kept this banner in hiding for a couple of centuries, waiting in the wings of history until He was ready to reintroduce it.

And reintroduce it He has!

This flag now hangs in thousands of homes, prayer rooms, sanctuaries, government buildings and even businesses. A church in Indiana made their own version—fifteen feet by thirty feet—then made me one! Another congregation decorated the Christmas tree in their foyer with dozens of small flags. Thousands of people have small ones tucked in their Bibles, tacked to bulletin boards, or conspicuously sitting on their desks. Others display them as lapel pins, wear them emblazoned on shirts, show them off on bumper stickers, and at least one person has the flag tattooed on his arm! Governors display the flag, as do judges and congressmen, and one was spotted in the U.S. Capitol. Another was recently flown over the Capitol of Arkansas. The other day I saw an appeal to heaven flag streaming behind an 18-wheeler—it's going viral!

The flag is associated with America's founding, to be sure. It seems that God doesn't intend it to be used by America alone, however. On this book's cover, it can be seen flying in the Himalayas—the highest point on the planet—where it is raised above dozens of Buddhist prayer flags. It has flown on the plains of Nineveh, the place of the first region-transforming revival, in South Africa, Panama, and more recently in Cambodia where it was used in prayers against human trafficking. Who knows where it will turn up next?! This international use seems especially appropriate, given America's God-given destiny of being a spiritual light to the nations.

Flags Carry A Message

In times past, flags carried more weight than they do in our present day. Their symbolism was understood, from the color to the design, enabling a flag to tell a story or make a strong statement. Many flags are sacred—people swear allegiance to them and die to protect their honor. Banners, as they are also called, were often intended to make declarations. One early colonial American flag had a picture of a coiled snake with the accompanying phrase, "Don't Tread On Me." It was a warning to Great Britain: "Be careful; step on us, and we strike!"

This journey of mine involves a different flag in America's past, one that is especially relevant to our God-given purpose and destiny. Modern day progressives, historical revisionists, liberal politicians, and humanistic professors would scoff at the notion that America was established by God for a divine purpose. They would also mock the assertion that our founders believed in and honored this divine-human partnership. As John Adams said, however, "facts are stubborn things...."[1] These modernists may not like our origins, but they can't change them. *Yahweh,* the God of the Bible, was indeed involved in America's founding, and He did so for His purpose.

When God brought the Appeal To Heaven flag into my journey, it launched me into another exciting chapter of my life calling: to see America experience a Third Great Awakening. This awakening, of course, isn't just for America; God doesn't love Americans more than any other group of people. This revival will sweep the world, becoming the greatest outpouring of the Holy Spirit since time began.

When General George Washington commissioned the Appeal to Heaven flag to fly over our naval ships in the Revolutionary War—don't look for that in our modern American History books—little did he know that 240 years later, God would ordain that it fly again. This time around, however, it won't fly over a fledgling nation being born, but over the most powerful nation in the world being *reborn*. This rebirth isn't literal, of course, but is a spiritual and moral renewal that will resurrect America's God-given calling, purpose and greatness.

It Is Not Too Late For America

Some Christian leaders teach, usually from theological influences, that America will not awaken, turn back to God and recapture her spiritual destiny. Their eschatology doesn't allow for a "comeback;" for them, the apostasy must continue to worsen.

Many secular leaders also contend, often with an ideological fervor fueled by their personal desires, that this rebirth will never occur. "America has 'progressed' too far," they assert with smug satisfaction, "having left behind its antiquated, puritanistic ideals and outdated beliefs." These naysayers are, indeed, correct when they euphorically and gloatingly bloviate about how far we as a nation have drifted from our original beliefs. Secularists and humanists are accurate when they condescendingly point out our moral shifts toward relativism and unbiblical values. With satisfied arrogance, these modernists gleefully vociferate that our government no longer sees itself under and accountable to an "imaginary" Creator, or even to an "outdated" Constitution He supposedly inspired.

It must, indeed, be acknowledged that America's populace is now filled with great apathy toward its history. It is also true that we are so ignorant of the ideals that shaped our identity as a nation that we have lost our national moorings. God's intent is that history be more than information; the past can be an important anchor. Without this stabilizing force, however, America is now adrift in a sea of secular experientialism, blown about by the wanderings of our own fantasies and the delirium they create. Truly, America's narcissistic independence from God has left us spiritually and morally bankrupt. We have searched for meaning apart from our Creator—a search which by definition must fail, for the purpose of any created thing can only be found in its creator— and are racing toward an even greater identity crisis of horrific proportions. With this loss of identity, America is experiencing a continuous drift from greatness to mediocrity and becoming increasingly irrelevant around the world.

All of these facts must be conceded.

I Have Great Hope

With such a dire diagnosis why, then, am I not hopeless? To the contrary, I have great hope for America because the depth of a fall never determines

God's ability to restore. I'm not afraid of the powerful strongholds because size and strength are completely irrelevant when measuring His ability to deliver. And I'm not intimidated because statistical odds, whether of success or failure, cease to be relevant when God is involved. His limitless ability negates the very concept of "odds," and trumps all other winning hands.

In the days of the flag's genesis, the American colonists had no chance of winning a war with the world's greatest empire, Great Britain. "Chance," however, lost its relevance once they chose an appeal to heaven over conceding to fate. When those ill-prepared and poorly equipped revolutionaries appealed for assistance to the Giver of inalienable rights, the tide turned. When they agreed to come under God's governance and honor His ways, He who "governs in the affairs of men," as Ben Franklin stated at the Constitutional Convention, did just that. Affirming the Lord's governing intervention, Franklin also said, "All of us who were engaged in the struggle must have observed frequent instances of super-intending providence in our favor."[2] Even some of our founders who were not strong Christians, such as Franklin, acknowledged God's providential hand in our victory.

And to prove it, they had put it on a flag.

That same "superintending providence" is available today. In spite of our many flaws and numerous failures, God's hand has been, and remains, on America. From the first man, Adam, to the Apostle Paul, history has proven that God uses imperfect people. The same is certainly true of nations. Though America is scarred and flawed, we still possess a divine purpose. Rest assured, the Sovereign who bestowed that purpose to America knows how to resurrect it.

Don't embrace any theology or creed that allows God to lose!

As you read this book, my prayer is that you will be awakened to hope. Hope is to the heart what seeds are to the earth. Without hope, life is sterile, unfruitful—dreams aren't conceived and destinies aren't realized. Hope is the starting line, the launch pad; it's the seedbed from which faith springs up, and a creative force that keeps the soul dreaming. Without doubt, the reemergence of this flag is intended by God to awaken hope.

I have hope, and I'm dreaming. I dream of a reborn America that is once again a shining light to the rest of the world. I believe this dream was born in God's heart, embedded in a small group of emigrant pilgrims, and is one I am confident He still maintains. Join me as I dream. Partner with the "superintending providence" that was active in our founding, is involved with our present, and has great plans for our future.

Let it be said of our generation that when a

nation teetered on the edge of destruction, having lost the ancient path of truth, we answered the divine call to war for its restoration. Let it be said of us as it was of our forefathers, that in the face of over-whelming odds, we took our stand in the celestial courtroom, appealing to the Judge of all the earth for His saving grace, mercy, and sustaining power.

Join the movement—*appeal to heaven!*

1

The Synergy Of The Ages

The Holy Spirit is an amazing and gracious teacher. Given the task of relaying incomprehensible things to fallible people, He does so with great skill, grace and patience. The Lord can drop entire ideas into our spirit in a moment of prayer, from a verse of scripture or at night in a dream. Other times, He gently takes us on a journey.

I am a man who has been on such a journey. Thirteen years ago, the Lord began speaking to me about the nature of time, and perhaps to prove His point, took an extended period of time doing so. In fact, if I had to guess, I'd say He's not done, although I understand His heart for it far more than I did when the journey began.

In 2001, I was asked to speak at Christ For The Nations Institute in Dallas, Texas. CFNI was dear to my wife Ceci and me because, in addition to receiving ministry training, it is the place where we first met in 1977. I went to CFNI looking for training and found a wife. What a deal! For many reasons, but specifically that one, CFNI will always be dear to my heart.

I love the heritage of CFNI. Founded in 1970 by Gordon Lindsay, the Bible school gave a training element to his love for the scriptures, his life of prayer, his heart for missions and evangelism, and his desire to further the signs and wonders movement that was taking place around the world. As a part of this latter tenet, Lindsay published the Voice of Healing magazine, recounting healings and revivals from across the nation and the world. Lindsay died in 1973, but CFNI continued to grow.

Agreeing With The Cloud Of Witnesses

As I spoke to the student body in 2001, I was concerned that CFNI was not walking in the fullness of what Gordon Lindsay had established. To be clear, it was not an issue of sin; the school was not in an apostate state. The institute was full of good administrators, faculty, and students who loved Jesus. I simply realized that just as happens to all of us from time to time, the institute was experiencing less than God intended it to experience and needed a stronger connection to its roots.

2

In response to this burden, I chose to replace one teaching session with a prayer meeting. The Lord can accomplish much more through prayer than any teacher can through teaching, and many times He will also bring great insight within that context.

As I led the student body in intercession, I heard the Lord whisper a phrase to me. "You need to agree in prayer with Gordon Lindsay." That startled me. Lindsay had died nearly 30 years earlier.

"Lord," I said, "is that really You speaking? He isn't here; he's in heaven." In retrospect, it's comical to try and explain something to the Lord, but I felt I needed to state the obvious.

"He's dead, Lord." I reiterated. "I can't bring him back to pray with him."

The response was simple, "But his prayers are not dead."

That idea rocked me. Now, if you had asked if I thought Gordon Lindsay's prayers had died with him, I would have said "no," but might have wondered if it were a trick question.

The Lord continued, "Until this generation comes into agreement with what Lindsay asked Me to do, I can't answer his prayer."

This greatly impacted me, as I realized God hadn't said, "I *won't*." He had clearly said that without this generation's agreement with Lindsay, "I *can't* answer his prayer." The idea of God saying He couldn't do something really turned my thinking on its ear.

Unfulfilled Promises

I began to ponder Hebrews 11, remembering the heroes of faith listed there along with some of their amazing exploits. Interestingly, however, the passage is also clear that some of those faith-heroes did not see the fulfillment of their promises. This has always seemed somewhat contradictory to me. When God searched history to accent great lives of faith, He chose to list some that did NOT receive the fulfillment of their God-given promises. These people went to the grave with unrealized promises from God, yet they had truly believed, even making it into the great Hall of Faith. Clearly, they weren't deficient in their walk of faith; why then did they die without seeing the promises fulfilled?

The last two verses of Hebrews 11 give us the amazing answer: they did not receive the fulfillment of their promises because *God wouldn't allow them to be complete without us.* That is incredible! We, today, play a role in these individuals' callings and assignments. The Greek word translated "complete" also means, "to finish; to mature; to reach the intended goal." Think about the ramifications of this: without us, God can't *finish* what He began through these saints; what He started through them cannot *mature*

4

or *reach its intended goal* until we grab the baton and run our leg of the race. That is mind-blowing!

God gave these individuals promises, but He didn't give them timelines. He did not tell them He would bring the fulfillment in their lifetimes, although I'm sure most of them expected Him to do so. The eternal God, who transcends time, speaks promises that are sometimes more reflective of His nature and relationship with time than ours. At times, He makes promises to people, knowing full well He will deliver on those promises through their children, grandchildren or spiritual descendants. I wonder what I may be finishing for some pastor or teacher from a few decades ago? Or perhaps even for some flag waving patriot warrior?

The generations are far more inter-connected than most of us realize. In God's mind, accomplishing something through our descendants is the same as doing it through us. Our comparatively shortsighted approach assumes every promise He makes will take place momentarily, or at the very least before we die! We can't fathom that a transcendent God might not share our urgency about the 80-year window we think of as life. Meanwhile, God feels no pressure, and understands that if He fulfills His promises through our offspring, the accomplishments were for us, as well as for them.

Conversely, the opposite is true. The scriptures tell us that the actions and accomplishments of individuals in former generations are sometimes credited to those who follow. Hebrews 7:9 states that the descendants of Levi paid tithes through their great, great grandfather Abraham. I wonder what blessing we're experiencing today that someone else paid for! There is an aspect of our spiritual walk that stretches beyond the boundaries of our window on earth. We can connect with things that occurred before us, and we can affect things that happen in the future. Our prayers know no bounds, so long as we are open to thinking about time from God's perspective, rather than our own. As I prayed at Christ For The Nations, I realized God was saying He couldn't do what He promised Gordon Lindsay *because He was waiting for us, the next generation, to do our part.*

The Synergy Of The Ages

But the Holy Spirit wasn't finished instructing me in this prayer session. He had a seven-word phrase with which He intended to rock my finite human mind. These seven words stretched my thinking yet again, and have resonated in me ever since: "I need the synergy of the ages."

"You need WHAT?" I immediately responded.

It is obvious by now that this prayer time was wreaking havoc on this teacher's preconceived concepts and paradigms! My 13-year journey was beginning with a series of theological brainteasers that, fortunately, were making me think outside of my God-limiting boxes.

What is the synergy of the ages? I quietly wondered.

Synergy is a fascinating concept. Think of it as a multiplication of power through combined effort. In almost all cases in the physical world, one plus one equals two. But not when people work together. When two or more people combine their efforts and strengths, power is multiplied—not just added. God so loves unity and agreement that He created a phenomenon through which power multiplies if we will simply work together!

Synergy doesn't just operate in the natural realm; it also exists in the spirit realm. Prayer is one example. Spiritual synergy takes place when two or more agree in prayer. The result is that through multiplied power much more is accomplished than would have been had we prayed alone. Leviticus 26:8 teaches us about this power of multiplication, "Five of you shall chase a hundred, and a hundred of you shall chase ten thousand, and your enemies shall fall before your sword." Spiritually, that's powerful; mathematically, however, it makes no sense. Think about it—if five of us can chase a hundred, that means each of us is responsible for twenty. At that rate, a hundred should chase two thousand, not ten thousand. But something unusual and supernatural takes place through agreement—synergy. When we agree in prayer, our power grows exponentially.

Synergy also occurs when generations connect. Honoring our parents multiplies our years on earth (Ephesians 6:1-3), while disconnecting from them brings forth curses (Malachi 4:6). Spiritual mantles, another word for callings and giftings, multiply in effectiveness through generational synergy (2 Kings 2:9). God's plan is always for the present generation to build on the strengths of the previous. This is the synergy of the ages—multiplied power through generational agreement and honor.

In Al Sanders' book, *Crisis in Morality!*, he compares descendants of an atheist, Max Jukes, to the offspring of a well-known preacher of that same era, Jonathan Edwards:

> *Max Jukes...married an ungodly girl and among their descendants were 310 who died as paupers, 150 as criminals, 7 as murderers, 100 as drunkards and more than half of the women were prostitutes.*

> *Jonathan Edwards...lived at the same time and married a godly girl. An investigation was made of 1,394 known descendants of theirs. Of these descendants, 13 became college presidents, 65 college professors, 3 United States senators, 30 judges, 100 lawyers, 60 physicians, 75 army and navy officers, 100 preachers and missionaries, 60 authors of prominence, one a vice-president of the United States, 80 became public officials...and 295 college graduates, among whom were governors*

of states and ministers to foreign countries.[1]

Could any testimony more powerfully make my point? Success, favor, and blessing can multiply down through the generations. But due to our ignorance in this area, we unknowingly break the generational storyline God is writing.

When the Holy Spirit spoke to me that day at CFNI, I was already aware of synergistic prayer. I knew I could agree in prayer with the person next to me and multiply power. I just didn't know I could agree with the generation behind me! Generational synergy—the synergy of the ages—was nowhere on my radar. Once God had awakened me to the principle, however, He wasn't about to stop with a Bible institute. Before He was finished, the Holy Spirit would challenge me to reach back to our nation's founders, agreeing with what He had birthed through them.

And when he did, a forgotten flag would be an important part of the process.

2

Put Yourself In The Storyline

Fear. Alarm. Curiosity. There's just something about an ambulance with its lights flashing that generates a strong mix of emotions. But seven of them! Something horrible must be occurring.

Fortunately, it was only a dream.

In the past, the Lord has frequently spoken to Julie Meyer, an internationally known worship leader and seasoned intercessor, through detailed dreams. In this dream, Julie saw seven ambulances lined up, each with lights flashing. Growing very concerned, she walked to the back of one of the ambulances to see what was happening. When she peeked in, Julie saw a non-responsive person laying on a gurney.

Next to the patient was an attendant working feverishly to revive him.

In her dream, Julie knew immediately this attendant was an angel, who looked at her and said, "I can't find a heartbeat." She went from one ambulance to the next, finding the same scenario—patients on gurneys with angels attending them, trying to restart their hearts. Suddenly, one of the angels looked directly at Julie and confided, "It's the intercessors."

This dream made sense to me. For a number of years, I have watched as the strength of the prayer movement has waned, many becoming weary. Intercessors have prayed years for revival, but the revival hasn't materialized, and many of them have experienced what Proverbs 13:12 refers to as "hope deferred." And as this passage teaches, hope deferred has made their hearts sick. Traveling across America, I can attest to the truthfulness of the dream. It's hard to find a heartbeat in many tired intercessors.

As Julie's dream continued, suddenly one of the angels shouted, "I found a heartbeat, but it's very faint!"

The other angels grew excited and asked, "What did you do?" They, of course, wanted to do the same thing in order to generate a heartbeat in their own intercessors.

The first angel replied, "Tell the old stories. When I started telling her stories of what God did in the past, her heart started to beat."

With that, these heavenly attendants began speaking to the intercessors about the First Great Awakening, the Second Great Awakening and other outpourings of the Holy Spirit—right up through the healing revivals and tent meetings of the 1940's, fifties and sixties. As they did so, the hearts of all the intercessors started beating again. At this point in the dream, an angel looked at Julie and directed her, "Tell the old stories of what God has done in the past."

As I first heard it, the entire dream was impacting, but this angelic messenger then added instructions that stirred my heart even more: "Tell the intercessors to put themselves in the storyline, because the old stories are also their stories." What a profound and intriguing thought!

Who among us really thinks this way? But we should. God has one overarching plan for humankind, not many; we're all part of the same unfolding drama. Our generation's role in history is simply another act of yesterday's play; our battles are conflicts of one ongoing war. Every revival in history is but a sequel in the Holy Spirit's ongoing series of outpourings, and every soul saved enters the same spiritual family. Our stories, though many, are one.

Put yourself in the storyline, because the old stories actually *are* your stories!

Synergy, Not Segmentation

For too long, we Christians—even those who are students of church history—have viewed accounts of past moves of God as something to be taken out of a box once in a while and dusted off for observation and sentimentality. We love those old stories, but we certainly don't think of them as something we can agree in prayer with, connect to, or draw strength from. And we've certainly never thought of them as "our" stories. They are past tense, a dead history. Just as I had never thought of Lindsay's story at CFNI as my story, I had never thought of Wesley and his Methodists as my movement. Finney's awakening certainly wasn't my awakening, and William Seymour's Azusa Street outpouring wasn't mine. Most of us simply don't think this way.

Our shortsighted reasoning has stolen from us the synergy of the ages. We've not put ourselves in the storyline. Since we don't typically align with past movements or agree with past prayers, this has all too often led to the *segmentation* of the ages, forcing each generation's intercession and effort to stand on it's own. Actually, the results are more devastating than that: God says that when the generations disconnect, it can create a curse (Malachi 4:6).

However, putting ourselves into the storyline God is writing allows us to tap into the strength and life of what He did years ago. We begin to understand the *eternal* purposes of God—not just the purposes we feel are for our present time. He then can continue through us what He began in someone else. And again, according to Hebrews 11:40, they can finally see their promise fulfilled.

This is what the Lord was trying to show me that day at Christ For The Nations. The student body and I needed to put ourselves into Lindsay's storyline, becoming a necessary link in the chain. We couldn't just assume God's promises to Lindsay would one day be fulfilled—the Holy Spirit needed agreement in order to finish what He had started. We had a vital role to play.

Reinforced by Julie's dream, this revelation opened my heart to a myriad of storylines we, as a generation, needed to identify with. We could insert ourselves into the storyline of Charles Finney, believing that city-changing revivals would be rekindled in our day. We could agree with the prayers of Rees Howells for revivals that would shake nations. We could join the efforts of Martin Luther King, Jr., and see his dream of racial healing in America reach its intended goal. The great cloud of witnesses had finally become more than mere spectators and cheerleaders to me; they were an earlier leg of a relay race, waiting for someone to grab their baton.

This truth pierced my conscience. God began the process of connecting my heart and actions with those who had lived before me. My life began expanding, being defined not just by an eighty or ninety-year destiny, but also by an inter-generational purpose. I realized I was part of a historical chain, planned by God and built with human lives. "Back to the future" took on new meaning: Like Elijah's servant, Elisha, I would have to connect with the past in order to find my future; the power he needed today was hidden in his yesterday (2 Kings 2:14-15). Reaching back would not only bring my life added significance, but also the lives of those who had lived before me (Hebrews 11:39-40). God's love of relational connection would find fulfillment, causing Him to release an entirely new level of spiritual power—the synergy of the ages.

Putting Myself Into America's Storyline

I immediately began processing this revelation in the context of my calling to America. It was obviously relevant to praying for nations. I knew I could connect with America's story more personally, joining my heart to the prayers and dreams of pilgrims, colonists, pioneers and every other generation that makes up our story. Whatever the cost, I determined to do my part in keeping the dream alive.

As I contemplated these connections, however, a problem began to surface in my thinking. I knew that some of America's story was painful and evil. Parts of the dream were more like a nightmare, a not-so-glorious past I would rather disconnect from. We are a nation of mortals, after all, with hearts of iron but feet of very muddy clay. How then do we deal with the muck?

Can we connect with our good history while pretending the bad doesn't exist? It seemed somewhat disingenuous to tout our great past, while overlooking our not-so-great portions. I was very aware of the pain embedded in the memories of various groups of Americans. Native and African Americans come to mind. Should we ignore their pain and expect them to simply "move on" or "get over it"? Obviously, this insensitive attitude only perpetuates their pain. That is not how God thinks. He doesn't want us to bury the pain, living in denial regarding the destructive part of our story; He wants to heal it.

The scriptures are filled with proof of this. David, an adulterous murderer, became the man after God's heart. Saul, a persecutor and killer of Christians, became the Apostle Paul. Rehab, the harlot, became a member of God's family and an inductee into His Hall of Faith (Hebrews 11:31). No, God doesn't deny the existence of evil in any of our pasts, but He does deny it the right—when repented of and turned from—to follow us into the future

Healing The Story

As the Lord began challenging me to enter America's story, He assured me that if I would do so, not only would He use me to continue it into the future, but also to heal portions of its past. If I was willing to identify with America's painful chapters, as well as her healthy ones, He would teach me how we can heal history. I remember the first time those words entered my mind: healing history. *What a wonderful thought,* I recall thinking, *but is that really possible?* I now know it is. History can never be changed, but it can be healed.

God wants all Americans, every race and creed, to know they are part of His plan for her. And He has every intention of melting the contents of the pot yet again, until we take on the flavor He, the Master Chef, is creating. Yes, that will require a lot of grace, understanding, and another level of healing. But we are, after all, appealing to heaven, home of the God who makes the impossible, possible.

3

Healing The Timeline

"That's not true!" I shouted out loud, though no one was present except yours truly. "How did that get in the Bible? Josiah was not the son of 'his father David,'" (2 Kings 2:22); "he was the son of a wicked King, Amon. In fact, David, the 'man after God's heart' lived several generations earlier," I continued, voicing my protest to God. I'm sure He was deeply concerned, as I pointed out a discrepancy in His history book, the Bible.

NOT!

My quest for truth not only eased my troubled mind; it also enlightened it. I discovered that David actually was a grandfather of Josiah, several generations removed. God allowed this young man, who "did right in the sight of the Lord" (2 Kings 22:2), to bypass his unrighteous fathers when referencing his ancestry, and leapfrog several generation back to David. *I'd rather be like David, a "man after God's heart,* Josiah must have thought, *than forsake the Lord, do evil, and worship idols as my fathers did* (2 Kings 21:20-22). *I'll just claim that as my heritage.*

It seems that God was more than just okay with this selective approach to his family tree; He most likely influenced Josiah to do so. Over a century earlier, Josiah's birth was prophesied, including his name, describing the reformation he would lead. "Behold, a son shall be born to the house of David, Josiah by name..." (1 Kings 13:2). That'll separate the grown-up prophets from the novices!

Problem solved.

Every family, race and nation has painful chapters in their story—points on the timeline with which we would rather *not* have a connection. America is no exception. As I sought the Lord regarding this, He began showing me that we, like Josiah, can disconnect from our ungodly past. Not only is it possible, but it is equally as important as connecting with the good.

To help me understand this, Holy Spirit led me to Hebrews 11:3, "By faith we understand that the worlds were prepared by the word of God, so that what is seen was not made out of things which are visible." A more literal Greek translation of the first half of this verse is, "By faith we understand that the ages (*aions*) have been properly connected or aligned (*katartizo*) by the spoken words of God..." (my rendering).

The Greek word I translated as "properly connected or aligned," *katartizo*, means "to put something into its proper position, alignment or connection." The "setting" of a broken bone was *katartizo*, as was the "relocating" of a dislocated joint; "mending" a torn net was, as well. The "restoration" of a fallen brother or sister in scripture is this word, too. Generally speaking, *katartizo* means to properly position a person or thing, whether at its inception or *as a restoration.*

Breaches In History

Interestingly, this verse in Hebrews 11:3 tells us God did this "positioning" with the ages or seasons of time. He declared the general flow of history and how each age would connect to the next. However, knowing the effects of Adam's sin and fallen humankind's consequent sinful nature, God also knew there would be dislocations and breaks in history's timeline. Like potholes after a hard winter, His original decreed connections would need seasons of repair. Pain would flow through history's breaches, creating the need for restoration and healing. He knew, for example, that innocent blood would be shed, abuses would transpire, idolatry would take place, covenants would be broken, slavery would occur, and a host of other sins would interrupt His original plan.

These breaches in the timeline would mandate restorations, reformations, and reconnections to His predetermined plan. Therefore, God not only declared the *aligning* of the ages, but where He knew it would be necessary, He also decreed their *realignment*—the healing of time. The fact that God heals history can be seen in Isaiah 58:12.

> *And those from among you will rebuild the ancient ruins; You will raise up the age-old foundations; And you will be called the repairer of the breach, The restorer of the streets in which to dwell.*

This verse clearly states that God heals— *Katartizo's*—history. As we stated in the previous chapter, He doesn't ignore the breaches in history and simply "move on." We humans engage in denial at times, because it seems to alleviate the pain, but God doesn't. His plan, as Isaiah said, is always to "rebuild...raise up...repair...restore" the broken time-lines. The mending of these breaks allows the pain of the past to heal, not be buried. Denial, as we know, only buries pain and causes the wound to fester. When this occurs, the pain will always resurface at some point in the future causing anger, violence, broken relationships and other expressions of dysfunctional behavior. Without true healing, this cycle of pain repeats itself generation after generation. Think of it as negative synergy.

Racism in America is a prime example. Because we have not known how to put ourselves into the storyline, allowing the Lord to heal and restore, pain is still flowing through our broken timeline. *Katartizo*, the realignment of the ages, hasn't occurred. Government tries to heal this breach through laws and programs, but this will never succeed. Individuals sometimes attempt it through denouncing and condemning the injustices and prejudices, but this too, fails. Other misguided people espouse the "get over it" or "move on" approach. Meanwhile, the wounds fester.

Government can never heal history's wounds, nor will its well-meaning laws and programs; the insensitive "get over it" crowd only offends, rubbing salt in an already painful wound; while the unhealed spokespersons of the wounded simply release more venom and hatred. These approaches only make the breaches worse.

In spite of the ineptitude of some to do so, however, Isaiah 58:12 makes clear that God does indeed use people to heal the breaches of history. "Those from among you..." is His plan. *Katartizo* is intended to happen through redeemed people as they understand and participate in prayer, fasting, confession of sin, and other spiritual activities. We are the peacemakers (Matthew 5:9). Through humility, repentance, God's love, and forgiveness, we can heal history's timeline. The Holy Spirit is bringing greater understanding of this process and we will effectuate it more skillfully in the coming season. As this occurs, and I know it will, people groups and cultures will be truly healed of yesterday's pain allowing God's life and blessing to flow through a *katartizo*'d joint in history.

I Stepped Into The Storyline

As this two-fold revelation regarding history grew in my heart and mind—connecting and disconnecting—for the first time I knew I could truly put myself into our nation's storyline. I was called to participate in the *katartizo*-ing of the ages, and I would do my part. America's history became alive and relevant to me—it was *my* history—one I could connect with, and when necessary, one I could help heal.

At this point in the journey, the Holy Spirit began sending me to numerous places around the country for both of these purposes. (Obviously and gratefully, I'm not the only one He has used in this way.) I visited dozens of historical sites significant in our country's founding and development, asking God to connect my heart with His original plan. I went to Washington D.C., many times. As I stepped into the storyline of my history as an American, I realized that my spiritual authority in the nation was increasing. My prayers and decrees were becoming more effective—the synergy of the ages was occurring.

I also traveled to many places where breaches had occurred in America's timeline, including locations representing broken covenants (treaties) with the Native Americans. I repented for our sins, often through many tears. I also visited ports of entry where slaves were brought into America and sold. I identified with the evil and repented for our sin, allowing God to break my heart over the painful atrocities. I traveled to battlefields where innocent blood was shed, to legislative chambers where unjust and unholy laws were passed, and to courtrooms where those immoral laws were upheld. I visited those places, not as a tourist, but as a participant and an intercessor. I repented for MY history, asking God to cleanse it with the blood of Jesus and heal the breach, so that blessing could once again flow through that link in history's chain.

I put myself into the *storyline*...to help heal the *timeline*.

To complete His process for me, in 2003 and 2004, I went to every state (I've since been to most of them numerous times). There is no part of this nation with which I haven't "connected" and to my knowledge, there is no part of its significant history—both the good and the bad—I haven't identified with spiritually.

I certainly don't share this to boast: indeed, I am but one of many who has participated in this identificational intercession. I say it to transparently point out a necessary process my all-too-calloused heart needed to experience, and to emphasize an immeasurably important and profound truth: *the path to the future is connected to the past...and that path runs through us!*

As this season of my journey came to an end, the Holy Spirit assured me that I, along with many others, had taken my place in America's storyline. I had become a link in His age-old chain and could now be part of His bridge to the future. Then, in 2007, He launched me into Phase Two of my journey. It came through a dream, a very remarkable dream. A dream about giants, a dream about America.

And a dream that would ultimately lead me to a very important flag.

4

Everlasting God

In 2007, I was speaking at a conference. A friend of mine was also there, and I knew God often spoke to him through dreams.

"Hey Thomas," I jokingly said as he headed toward his room, "Ask God to give you a dream for me tonight."

"Okay," he replied in the same lighthearted manner.

The next morning, to my surprise, the first words out of Thomas' mouth were, "Hey Dutch, God gave me a dream about you last night!"

My first thought was, *Wow. I wish it were always this easy!* Something about laying my head on a pillow and waking up with a word from the Lord whenever I wanted sounded especially appealing.

He continued. "In the dream, you were a boxer. You faced five giants in five rounds and knocked each of them out—one each round. You knocked each one out with one punch; and with each giant, you alternated fists. The first giant was floored with a right, the second with a left, back and forth you went until they were all down for the count. Five giants, five rounds, five punches, alternating fists."

"After you knocked out the fifth giant," Thomas continued, "you walked out of the ring and directly up to me. Holding up your gloved fists, you declared, 'If you're going to take out the giants in this season, you're going to have to wear these two gloves. One of the gloves had the word 'Everlast' on it; the other read 'Evergreen.' "

Fascinating.

Everlasting God

The name on the first glove made total sense to me, both in relation to boxing and to spiritual warfare. Everlast is one of the most common names in boxing equipment. Any boxing match you have ever seen probably featured Everlast gear. Everlast began in the early 1900's as a sporting goods equipment company focused on making long-lasting swimwear.

In 1917, a young boxer named Jack Dempsey asked them to make boxing gear, including gloves and headgear that would last through fifteen rounds of punishment. Two years later, Dempsey won the heavyweight championship using Everlast gloves, and overnight they became the standard for serious fighters. Almost a hundred years later, if you're going to do business in the boxing ring, you probably do so with Everlast equipment. There really is no viable competition. As their slogan decries, "We Are Fight Sports."[1]

The word "Everlast" meant more to me than just boxing equipment, however. I knew there was a scriptural connection, and I knew what it was. True to form, the Lord had been paving the way for me so I would recognize it at the right time. In that season, I had been studying the life of Abraham and his journey with God. In Genesis 21:33, scripture tells us that Abraham called on "the Everlasting God." The name in Hebrew is *Olam El*, and it's the first time in scripture anyone used that phrase as a name for God.

In biblical times, the meaning of an individual's name was important, often referring to a person's calling, nature or some other identifiable characteristic. This is the reason God has so many names and why He sometimes changed a person's name, as He did with Abraham (Genesis 17:5).

First time introductions of people and ideas are also important. Think about introducing someone—

you tend to try and give context to the person meeting him or her. You may say, "This is my father, George" or "Meet my boss, Frank." You may even clarify who they are in a way that fits the situation. For example, if a friend wants to build a home and you're trying to help them, you might choose to add details, saying, "This is my father, George, a builder." Because your friend needed to know a homebuilder, you pointed out that facet of your father's identity. An introduction often says a lot about whom that person is, and scripture follows this protocol.

The Timeless God

Consistent with this principle, when Abraham called on God in this passage, he used a new name because the Lord had revealed Himself in a new way. The name *Yahweh* is powerful but didn't convey that revelation. *Elohim* and *Adonai* are amazing names of God, yet this situation required something different, something...everlasting.

Even the translation, "Everlasting God," is not quite enough to describe the full meaning of *Olam El*. The *El* portion of the name means strong, mighty, or powerful. But *Olam* is much more challenging to define; its meaning is greater than simply "as far as possible into the future." *Olam* actually extends both directions in time. It is forward and backward—forever! One lexicon described *Olam* as the most distant times in both directions. Even that falls short, however, because the word "times" in the definition violates the very concept of *Olam*. The concept of *Olam* is not confined to a timeline, and neither is God; the Everlasting God exists outside of time. If you were to go back to the very beginning of time, He was before that. *Olam El* defies definition!

The way humankind thinks about time forces us to consider a start and a finish. *Olam El*, however, knows no beginning or end. When time as we know it comes to a close, the Ancient of Days will continue. He sees the past, present, and future—all at once. Obviously, this enables Him to have a unique perspective, seeing the results of an action long before it happens (for example, Adam's fall and the consequential need of the cross); it also gives God the unique ability to deal with the ramifications of events that occurred in the past, erasing their consequences as though the events never took place. For example, God doesn't see a born-again, former prostitute as "a former prostitute;" He doesn't see the redeemed murderer as "a former murderer." God separates our sins from us "as far as the east is from the west," (Psalm 103:12) and remembers them no more (Hebrews 8:12, 10:17). *Olam*, through the cross, eradicates all records of our former sins. In Abraham's day, He did so through other offerings and sacrifices.

Abraham And Everlasting God

Consider Abraham's situation when he calls on the Lord as *Olam El*, Everlasting God. Abraham has been on a twenty-five year journey of faith and as he looks back over that timeline, he can see places where he failed miserably. Not being perfect, he could see blotches, torn places, and embarrassing failures on his timeline.

Most believers think of Abraham as "the father of faith," a description of him taken from Romans 4:16. Likewise, Hebrews 11 refers to him as a great man of faith. We forget, however, that Abraham wasn't a great faith-man his entire life. There were significant deviations from that path. Romans 4:20 references this when it says Abraham "*grew* strong in faith" (italics added).

Actually, Abraham and Sarah both wavered at times in their faith that God would give them a son. The Lord had promised them children, but when no children came, their lack of faith in God's promise caused them to introduce Hagar into the family, resulting in the birth of Ishmael. Later, they actually laughed a cynical laugh at God's final re-stating of the promise. And why not? Abraham was 99 years old and Sarah was 90 (Genesis 17: 1, 17).

This wasn't Abraham's only failure of faith, however. On two different occasions when Abraham and Sarah were younger, he was afraid that foreign kings might kill him in order to marry her. His solution for these predicaments included the despicable acts of pretending Sarah was his sister instead of his wife. In essence, he threw Sarah to the wolves in order to save his own life. She was, indeed, taken by the kings but God supernaturally intervened before physical unions occurred. These connivings were horrible breaches of the marriage covenant and bold-faced lies—ones I'm sure necessitated some awkward conversations with kings when Abraham had to later set the record straight. He and Sarah probably had a few things to work out, as well!

Everlast Heals The Past

So why does the Bible call Abraham a father of faith and a friend of God? Because even though he may not have fulfilled these descriptive phrases at every step of the journey, they are accurate descriptions of how he finished. Abraham isn't remembered by God as "the former covenant breaker," "the one-time liar," or "the double-minded man." He is God's friend and our faith example! Abraham was grateful his past actions were not allowed to define his present situation. *Olam El* had navigated him through every season— even the embarrassing ones—and preserved his destiny. And as He does for all of us, He reached back in time and cleansed Abraham's wrongs, once and for all.

With that in mind, one can almost see Abraham as he searches for the right name to use in thanking and glorifying *Elohim*. Finally, exhausting all known possibilities, he has to create a new one. The declaration may have been something similar to this:

> *You are more than* Yahweh, Adonai *and* Elohim. *You are the infinite and powerful God of the Ages*—Olam El! *You are outside of time and Lord over time! As Ruler over the past, present and future, you healed my breaches and kept my destiny intact! When I was unfaithful, You were faithful; when I doubted, You overcame my unbelief; when I lied, You were able—not only to forgive me—but to cleanse me and keep my marriage intact. And even when our bodies were too old to conceive and reproduce—99 and 90 years of age! —You placed some of Your timeless nature in Sarah and me, and we drank from the fountain of youth! Truly, You are the creator of and ruler over time—Everlasting God!*

With that declaration, Abraham entered a new phase in his walk with *Yahweh*. He recognized that the God who was bigger than his past could be fully trusted with his future. Abraham desperately needed this revelation, having been promised land he did not yet have and descendants that did not yet exist. He had been promised a nation, but a nation had yet to rise up. He and Sarah were now old. But Abraham laid hold of *Olam El,* the God who could bring his fractured past into alignment and chart the right course for his destiny-driven future.

In the last chapter, we mentioned the God who *katartizo*'s the ages healing the breaches of history (Hebrews 11:3). *Olam El* is that God. He knows how to reach back into the most difficult of life's seasons and redeem them, expertly removing offenses and reshaping our hearts. He snaps our lives back into alignment, healing our history and promising us a hope-filled future.

America's Everlasting God

When I pray for revival in America I boldly and confidently wear this glove mentioned in the dream. I know well the breaches in our history—the injustices, the evil acts and our many sins. Like Abraham, we have failed, sometimes egregiously. But I also know *Olam El* and what He can do through the blood of the cross. No giant is too big for Him.

At times, I am challenged by individuals contending that God cannot send revival to America and restore her destiny. "Our sins and evils are just too great," they tell me.

I remind them of Abraham.

Yes, our nation has a flawed past and perhaps an even more flawed present. But I'm not asking for a merit-based revival where God gives us tokens of His goodness in response to our excellent behavior. Obviously, God isn't going to award America with a revival simply because He's impressed with our actions. But isn't that the point of revival? If we were "good enough," we wouldn't need one!

I'm asking for awakening because covenant-keeping *Olam El* lives up to His name. I'm asking for revival because I know the timeless God can reach back and heal our breaches. Everlasting God can *katartizo* those events and our hearts, repairing the wrongs we're responsible for and also the ones we've inherited. Forgiveness and cleansing—redemption—are specialties of His. When *Olam* does this, blessings can and will flow through our timeline once again.

At an earlier time in our nation's history, another Abraham reached out to *Olam* for healing and mercy. President Lincoln, facing one of the darkest times in our country's existence, knew our only hope for survival was a massive, national appeal to heaven. His proclamation was profound. Read it carefully:

> *...And whereas it is the duty of nations as well as of men to own their dependence upon the overruling power of God, to confess their sins and transgressions in humble sorrow, yet with assured hope that genuine repentance will lead to mercy and pardon, and to recognize the sublime truth, announced in the Holy Scriptures and proven by all history, that those nations only are blessed whose God is the Lord.*

And, insomuch as we know that by His divine law nations, like individuals, are subjected to punishments and chastisements in this world, may we not justly fear that the awful calamity of civil war which now desolates the land may be but a punishment inflicted upon us for our presumptuous sins, to the needful end of our national reformation as a whole people? We have been the recipients of the choicest bounties of Heaven; we have been preserved these many years in peace and prosperity; we have grown in numbers, wealth, and power as no other nation has ever grown. But we have forgotten God. We have forgotten the gracious hand, which preserved us in peace and multiplied and enriched and strengthened us, and we have vainly imagined, in the deceitfulness of our hearts, that all these blessings were produced by some superior wisdom and virtue of our own. Intoxicated with unbroken success, we have become too self-sufficient to feel the necessity of redeeming and preserving grace, too proud to pray to the God that made us!

It behooves us, then, to humble ourselves before the offended Power, to confess our national sins, and to pray for clemency and forgiveness...

All this being done in sincerity and truth, let us then rest humbly in the hope authorized by the divine teachings that the united cry of the nation will be heard on high and answered with blessings no less than the pardon of our national sins and the restoration of our now divided and suffering country to its former happy condition of unity and peace...[2]

What a powerful appeal to heaven! Many in our government today do not agree with Lincoln or with the "Holy Scriptures" he referenced. They would scoff at the assertion "that those nations only are blessed whose God is the Lord." Having "forgotten God," we are now much like the America Lincoln described. But the God who saved us then can save us now.

We must pray intently, in agreement with the appeals of our forefathers and predecessors, in order to see a continuation of what they birthed. And we must actively repent of our wrongs and theirs, allowing God to reach back in time, healing our history so that blessings can flow into our present.

Olam El, Everlasting God, made perfect sense as the meaning of one of the boxing gloves that would serve to knock out the giants we face. Understanding His timeless and redeeming nature will cause us to pray differently about the past and the future. We can confidently repent of history's sins and unwaveringly agree with history's promises. *Olam El* eagerly awaits these redemptive prayers.

Thomas' dream didn't end with Everlast, however. The other boxing glove was marked Evergreen. Though I prayed and studied, the meaning of this one remained a mystery for a while...a long while. By the time the Lord revealed it, I had moved on to other things. But true to His nature, He brought the understanding.

And when it finally came, it was wrapped in a flag.

5

Evergreen

It was May 2013, and I was at the graduation ceremony of Christ For the Nations Institute—back at the "synergy of the ages" location. Six years had gone by since the boxing dream. I understood the Everlast glove, but the meaning of its counterpart, Evergreen, had evaded me so long it was now relegated to the Rarely-Ever-Think-About-It file in my brain. Not that I had ceased caring; it had just been so long that I rarely thought about it.

As the Executive Director of the Institute, it was my responsibility to choose the commencement speaker. I chose one of my spiritual sons, not because he's a great preacher, but because he isn't a preacher at all. Bill is a military man—a JAG attorney for a branch of our Special Forces. As an attorney, he was not required to participate in some of the intense training Special Forces' soldiers endure, but Bill chose to anyway. His desire was to be a full-on soldier, not only an attorney, and Bill has proven his mettle time and time again. He actually once told me in a playful manner, "I love you, Papa Dutch, but I could kill you in six seconds."

I stopped calling him "Son" and started calling him "Sir!"

I chose a soldier as our commencement speaker because I wanted our graduates to know they did not have to be a pastor or preacher in order to have a calling from God. All believers are called to serve God—regardless of the gifting He gave them and the sphere in which they minister. Also, I wanted the students to hear from someone who modeled honor, integrity, and sacrifice—character traits the young people in our society today hear far too little about. Bill did an outstanding job in his address.

The Gift

At the end of his message, however, this young man threw me a bit of a curve. "I believe the Lord has asked me to give a special gift to Papa Dutch," he said. I wasn't sure about this, not wanting the emphasis to move from the graduates to me. But he had the microphone and, after all, could have killed me in 6 seconds.

I decided to trust him!

"Before I give you the gift," he said, "I need to explain the history behind it. It's a replica of the flag displayed by George Washington and America's founding fathers. This flag was actually used before the Stars and Stripes existed. In many ways, it is the banner under which America was born," he explained.

I must add that neither Bill nor I would ever allow any flag to displace "Old Glory" in our hearts and actions—I display her proudly and still tear up during the Pledge of Allegiance. Nonetheless, the symbolism of this earlier flag is extremely important.

Appeal To Heaven

"This banner has the phrase 'An Appeal To Heaven' across the top," he continued, "a phrase our Founders took from the writings of John Locke, an influential English philosopher from the mid-1600's. Locke wrote a series of papers on 'Natural Laws,' stating that human rights originate with God, not government."

Locke made the case that when people have done everything humanly possible to experience those God-given rights and have failed to do so, there remains but one option:

And where the body of the people or any single man, is deprived of their right, or is under the exercise of a power without right, and have no appeal on earth, then they have a liberty to appeal to heaven...[1]

Bill continued, "Locke's phrase, 'appeal to heaven,' connotes that when all resources and the ability to attain justice on earth are exhausted, an appeal to earth's ultimate Judge is the final recourse. This concept would become a foundational philosophy in American society, used even in the Declaration of Independence."

Bill went on to explain that George Washington and his contemporaries grabbed hold of this phrase in America's cause for freedom from Britain's tyranny. Having exhausted all peaceful possibilities of experiencing the liberty they so desired, the colonists realized their only hope for freedom was through war. Yet with Britain's great military, weaponry, and wealth, contrasted by the colonist's dire lack of these resources, any military attempt to break free from British rule was preposterous, even laughable. Laughable, that is, unless Almighty God intervened.

The stance of the colonists was simple. Their right to freedom came from God; He would help them. "We will appeal to heaven!" they declared.

And a flag was born.

God's Dream For America

From the days of the pilgrims, godly men and women have believed the Almighty was involved in the birth of our nation. They also felt that if a nation chose to partner with and honor God, it would experience His favor and blessing in extraordinary ways. Washington and the colonial dreamers agreed. But they decided to take it a step farther and find out if the Sovereign was, indeed, birthing "a city [nation] set on a hill that can't be hidden...a light to the world," (Matthew 5:14). They no doubt knew of John Winthrop, a leader of the puritan's Massachusetts Bay Colony, using this verse in his 1630 speech on board the Arbella to describe what he believed God wanted to build in America.[2]

They knew of the planting of the cross at Cape Henry in 1607, and of the ensuing prayer meeting dedicating the land to His glory. They had read the Mayflower Compact of 1620, stating the voyage was made "for the glory of God, and advancement of the Christian faith..."[3] Would God honor these events and prayers? Even more importantly, was He inspiring these actions? Was America God's dream? They believed it was indeed.

The pilgrims absolutely believed America had a God-given destiny, and our founding fathers did, as well. Throughout our history, America's presidents and leaders have reiterated this belief. John F. Kennedy referenced Matthew 5:14 and Winthrop's famous speech, as did Ronald Reagan and numerous other U.S. Presidents.[4] Though modern day revisionists try to rewrite and remove our history, the truth will always trump their lies.

General George Washington, leader of the American Revolution, obviously believed in this divine plan. He commissioned several ships for the Revolutionary War efforts and, highlighting their dependence on providential help, each vessel was to fly under the Appeal to Heaven banner, also known as the Pine Tree Flag.[5] The popularity of the flag spread and was soon flying throughout the colonies, as well as being adopted as the flag for the Massachusetts state navy.[6] It became the symbol of these colonists' unwavering spirit of liberty, as well as a clear statement of where they placed their faith.

The Evergreen

Bill's explanation of the appeal to heaven phrase and its connection to our past was very meaningful to me, but the impact was about to intensify. One never knows when the Lord is about to sneak up on them. The Apostle Paul was blindsided by the Holy Spirit—literally—losing his sight for a few days so he could see the true light; Jonah took a ride in a "chartered" fish in order to deliver God's message to Nineveh; and Moses had his destiny reinstated through a conversation with a fireproof burning bush! I know—makes your head spin. Mine wasn't as dramatic as

Moses', but God WAS about to speak to me from a tree.

"They put an evergreen tree on this flag," Bill continued, as he unfurled it and held it up for me to see. When I saw the Appeal to Heaven flag, the presence of the Lord engulfed me. And suddenly... I remembered the dream. A six-year wait was coming to an end, an old evergreen was about to be resurrected, and a 250-year-old flag was about to be reborn. With a genuine sense of reverence and excitement I realized, *I've just been given the other glove.*

What is the significance of the evergreen tree? Always maintaining green leaves or needles, depending on the tree, evergreen trees have symbolized *eternity*, as far back as Abraham.

At times, this "eternal" symbolism was expanded to include *an everlasting or life-long commitment to a covenant.* At the time of our nation's founding, evergreens carried this significance to the Iroquois Native American nation. At a significant time in their history, a great leader united five native tribes (with a later addition of a sixth) establishing a confederacy among them. According to the Iroquois Constitution, their covenant began with the planting of the "Tree of Peace." Their peace treaty and everlasting covenant was then sealed by the symbolic act of burying weapons underneath a great evergreen tree.[7] Some historians believe this covenantal ceremony is where we get the phrase, "bury the hatchet."

The Iroquois' government and some of their cultural traditions were very influential to our founders. Benjamin Franklin was perhaps the greatest advocate of the Iroquois Nation being an example for the American Colonies. Franklin, who first published the image of the serpent with the words "Join or Die" in his Pennsylvania newspaper, also published several works containing the proceedings of Native American councils. And in 1751, Franklin wrote a letter in which he purported that if longstanding unity could work for the Iroquois, why not the American Colonies:

> *It would be a strange thing if [these] Six Nations...should be capable of forming a scheme for such an union, and be able to execute it in such a manner as that it has subsisted ages and appears indissoluble; and yet that a like union should be impracticable for ten or a dozen English colonies, to whom it is more necessary and must be more advantageous, and who cannot be supposed to want an equal understanding of their interests.[8]*

Franklin's Albany Plan for uniting the colonies was also based on the structure of the Iroquois government.[9] The influence of the Iroquois Nations on the founding of the U.S. government was significant enough that in 1988 the Senate passed a resolution "To acknowledge the contribution of the Iroquois

Confederacy of Nations to the development of the United States Constitution."[10]

Some historians believe that due to the Iroquois' influence, the "eternal" and "covenantal" evergreen was placed on the Appeal to Heaven flag as a symbol of our nation's covenant with God, and possibly of our Founders' commitment to one another. This is consistent with the spirit of covenant they demonstrated when pledging "our Lives, our Fortunes and our sacred Honor" to one another and the cause.[11] Certainly, the Appeal to Heaven phrase on the flag supports this belief that the evergreen tree is also related to our alliance with and dependence on God.

Abraham And The Evergreen

As significant as the Iroquois connection is, however, the evergreen's use as a picture of eternal fidelity to covenant didn't originate with them. The most important and weighty example of this symbolic use goes all the way back to Abraham and his covenant with *Yahweh.* In Genesis 21:33, Abraham called on *Olam El,* the Everlasting God. I had already realized, when presented with the dream in 2007, the understanding behind this name was the meaning of the "Everlast" glove. But imagine my surprise when shortly after receiving the flag I discovered that before calling on *Everlast*, Abraham planted an *evergreen* tree. Obviously, I had read this verse often enough to remember that Abraham planted a tamarisk tree before calling on *Olam El*. I just didn't know a tamarisk tree was an evergreen! He planted an *evergreen tree* and called on the *Everlasting God*. Abraham wore both gloves.

Pardon my Texas slang, but—you can't make this stuff up!

When I discovered this, I was astounded. Only God could hide a message to a nation in an ancient verse of scripture regarding our father of faith Abraham, and unpack it through a strange dream about knocking out 5 giants, in 5 rounds, using un-matching boxing gloves.

Amazing.

Why did Abraham plant the evergreen tree? Memorials or monuments were extremely important in Abraham's day, used to remind people and nations of significant events. When Abraham planted the evergreen tree, he was establishing a witness or memorial to his covenant relationship with Everlasting God. The tree's message was: "*Olam* has proven Himself faithful to His covenant with me time and time again. I now declare my covenant faithfulness to Him. I will forever honor my covenant with Everlasting God."

Abraham's choice of evergreens is interesting. I have read numerous articles describing the tamarisk tree. Three significant facts, among many, are that it is *slow-growing, long-living,* and when fully-grown *produces cool shade.* Because the tree is so slow-growing, no one would plant a tamarisk for him or herself; he or she would never personally benefit from it. By planting this particular evergreen, Abraham was thinking of his descendants, making a powerful declaration to them for generations to come, "I am in covenant with *Olam,* and you can sit under the shade of this everlasting covenant."

Wow!

When we live in covenantal faithfulness to God, not only are we blessed but our children and grandchildren are, as well. This has certainly been the case with America. We have been extremely blessed by the God-connections of the generations before us. But each succeeding generation must also honor God and His word. When the Holy Spirit mentioned "Evergreen" in the boxing dream, then connected it to the flag under which America was born, He was pointing America back to covenant with Him. If we would once again honor our promises to *Yahweh,* returning to the God of our fathers; if we would return to God's original purpose and plan for America, partnering with Him in His cause of redemption throughout the world; then the faithfulness of Everlasting God would be demonstrated to us, delivering us from the giants ravaging our land.

The American Dream

The original American dream wasn't about wealth, but freedom—freedom to worship and freedom from tyranny. It was also about partnering with God to release the light of His word to all nations, and exporting His glorious gospel to the ends of the earth. It was a shared dream, born in the heart of God and deposited in the womb of our nation. But America has perverted this holy desire and God-honoring partnership, turning the dream into a narcissistic lust for money, possessions and pleasure. As uncontrolled appetites always do, our gluttonous cravings gradually grew in intensity until we no longer controlled them—they controlled us. Liberty became license; independence became rebellion; and our "freedoms" enslaved us. Of course, at some point the piper—which for us became the discordant notes of our perverted dream—will always demand his payment. And now, we are no longer feeding on the dream; the dream is feeding on us.

Our mutated dream has enslaved us to the "giants" spoken of in the boxing dream. The giant of debt, in and of itself, could destroy America. The wealthiest nation on earth has borrowed its way out of freedom and into bondage. Other giants in our land—abortion, violence, racism, numerous addictions and sexual perversions—all are strongholds ruling and destroying America.

It doesn't stop there. Our government is in

complete chaos, having lost the ability to govern even with simple common sense, let alone wisdom and accurate constitutional law. Black-robed ideologues found the right to abortion in one word, "privacy," in our Constitution. What intellectually honest person wouldn't acknowledge the ignorance and hypocrisy of that? But "legislating from the bench" has become the accepted way for liberals to reshape America.

Many of our leaders now deny America's true history and oppose her Creator. Our current president contends that we have always been a Muslim, as well as Christian, nation and that Islam was significant in our founding. If the majority in our media and education system had enough character, these absurd lies would be both exposed and scoffed at. They, however, now honor preference above truth, ideology above integrity. Their means now justifies their desired end, which is a new and radically different America where God is mocked, His ways are scorned and amorality is the new law of the land.

Many of our churches, which are supposed to carry the antidote for this poison, are now lukewarm, if not totally apostate. Uncertain about the Bible, these congregations now wallow in the same relativism they're supposed to be a standard against. Having become sub-cultures, not counter-cultures, they change nothing. No Bible-believing Christian who understands the wages of sin could deny that America is in desperate trouble.

Is There Hope For America?

Our spiritually-sick and nationally-weak condition, then, begs the sobering questions: Is there hope for America? Can we find our way back to greatness, reconnecting to the God that made us great? Will we find "the old paths...the good way" (Jeremiah 6:16), and once again experience the favor and blessing of our Creator?

Yes, if we sucker-punch the giants!

We will win if we, like Abraham and our forefathers, connect to Everlast. If we return to a faith that God and His redeeming power are bigger than our weaknesses and failures, we will defeat the over-fed giants of our day. If we can believe that through the blood of Jesus, God's mercy triumphs over judgment (James 2:13), and that He who began a good work in us can finish it (Philippians 1:6), we'll prevail.

Then we must dust off the other glove, Evergreen. If we return to covenant with the God of our fathers, embracing the destiny He planned for us, *Olam* will deliver us from the spiritual giants robbing us of our calling and inheritance.

Can we find these two gloves? Absolutely. The process has already begun. A remnant—and God always begins with a remnant—has already been appealing to heaven for help. God is about to respond to these prayers with a Third Great Awakening. This heaven-sent revival will restore the gloves to millions more who will step into the ring properly equipped. The God of 2 Chronicles 7:14 is about to manifest Himself:

> *[If] My people who are called by My name humble themselves and pray and seek My face and turn from their wicked ways, then I will hear from heaven, and will forgive their sin and will heal their land.*

Rest assured, the God who loves to save is listening to our prayers with favor. We are not trying to twist the arm of a reticent God, talking Him into doing something He would rather not do. Remember the story of the prodigal son. It was not the prodigal's father—who no doubt pictures God—that was hesitant to forgive and restore. It was the self-righteous brother. The merciful and loving father *ran* to the returning prodigal (Luke 15:11-32). That's the God we're appealing to!

Like the prodigal's brother, many in the religious community today don't believe God is willing to forgive and heal America. Unbiblical in their beliefs, they somehow believe God would rather judge than save. But our God loves to save! Though uncompromisingly righteous, He was more than willing to spare Sodom for the sake of only ten righteous individuals (Genesis 18:32). Never discount the power of God's redeeming love.

Appeal to heaven!

One More Dream

As I began processing this wonderful ancient flag and my newfound, giant-killing gloves, God, in His determined attempt to make sure I had the full message, gave one more dream...and what an amazing dream it was.

6

Are You Ready?

There are dreams, and then there are dreams. When I receive one of my rare God-dreams, as opposed to those inspired by pizza and Tex-Mex, sometimes I feel like I've matured into the Major League of prophetic revelation. Then I hear about a REAL dream, given to a TRUE dreamer, and I realize I'm still in T-ball. The following dream was a Major League grand slam.

Given by the Holy Spirit to my friend, Rick, the dream seemed to encapsulate my 13-year journey: the synergy of the ages; putting ourselves into the storyline; the fact that God was involved in the birth of America; and the significance of the Appeal to Heaven flag.

In the dream, Rick found himself in an old wooden tabernacle, much like those found years ago on Christian campgrounds. It was dark inside and as he looked for lights, an elderly man approached, asking if he'd like a tour. Rick and I believe the "old man" represented *Olam*, the everlasting God and Ancient of Days.

The first thing this heavenly "tour guide" did was turn on all the lights and open all the windows, which were large pieces of hinged plywood, held open by poles. As the auditorium filled with light, Rick could see that it was huge, seating twenty-five to thirty thousand people. The gentleman then escorted my friend to the platform and instructed him to sit on a stool.

America's Generations

"Look out those windows," he said, pointing to the east. As Rick looked, he saw ships approaching in the distance. *Those look like pilgrim ships,* he thought. Sure enough, they were. Three thousand or more people from that generation of Americans disembarked, made a procession into the tabernacle, took their seats, and began worshipping God.

"Now, look out those windows," the man instructed, pointing in a different direction. As Rick looked, he saw pioneers coming in the distance— women in long skirts and bonnets, covered wagons pulled by oxen and other items depicting the era.

Just as the pilgrims had, three to four thousand pioneers made a procession into the tabernacle while the previous generation stood and cheered: "Well done! Thank you for your hard work. Thanks for keeping the dream alive..." When all the pioneers were inside, both generations began worshipping.

After a few moments, the host approached again, "Look out those other windows." Sure enough, another generation of Americans was approaching. "These are the planters," he said. "They built the roads, railroads, towns, and cities." Just as the other generations had, they processed into the tabernacle to loud cheers from the previous groups. When they were inside, all three generations stood, and fervent worship ascended.

This scene repeated itself with three more generations of Americans approaching and entering the tabernacle. Six generations in total were now present, twenty thousand or more strong, all worshipping. "The praise was so loud," Rick told me later, "the building was shaking."

At this point, the dream's host approached yet again, pointing to a seventh set of windows. As Rick watched, people from our era moved toward the building in cars and trucks. Just as the others, they made their entrance into the gathering—to great cheers, followed by passionate worship.

The Delegates

Seven generations of Americans now stood worshipping together, literally causing the building to vibrate from the sound of their praise. After a few moments, the older man approached my friend yet again. "Watch these double doors," he instructed. As Rick looked, a representative from the pilgrims entered, walked up to the center of a bridge arching over the platform and began to prophesy God's plans and purposes for America. The people listened quietly as for several minutes he declared her corporate destiny, after which the worship ensued.

Five more times this was repeated—delegates from six generations decreeing and prophesying over America, each one followed by more worship. Finally, when the time came for our generation to decree, the pattern changed. Approaching my friend with a very serious demeanor, the old man asked him a penetrating question, "Are you ready to take your place in the synergy of the ages?"

As you can imagine, hearing this phrase—that was first spoken to me in 2001—astonished me. Interrupting his account, I inquired," Before the dream, had you ever heard this phrase? Have you heard me or anyone else ever mention the synergy of the ages?"

"Never," he assured me, as I stared at him in stunned silence.

This phrase, along with the fact that each generation of Americans was present, clearly pointed to the synergy created through multi-generational agreement. Seven generations; one nation. Many lives; one story.

The fact that the phrase came in the context of a question is also significant: *"Are you ready to take your place...?"* It seems to me that God is asking an entire generation of American believers that question: "Will you join the appeal?" Each one will have to answer for her or himself. My prayer is that you take up the cause. We need you.

Continuing his account of the dream, Rick related his emphatic answer to the old man's question, "Yes, I'm ready to take my place."

"Go through the door and join the other leaders from your generation," he was told.

Unlike the previous generations, ours had numerous representatives, many of whom he recognized. Together, they all marched into the room and took their seats. All of them, that is, except the last one in line. He, instead, headed toward the bridge.

The Flag

"You were the last one, Dutch," he told me, causing the hair on the back of my neck to stand up! "You were the delegate from this generation. As you climbed the bridge, I noticed that unlike the other delegates, you were carrying something in your hands. When you reached the center, you began unfolding a white flag."

I was almost afraid to believe what might be coming. My mind was racing. *Is he about to describe the flag that has just been given me—the Appeal to Heaven flag?* Before he could continue I blurted out, "Did it by any chance have the words 'An Appeal to Heaven' on it?"

It was now Rick's turn to be surprised. Having never seen or heard of the flag before his dream, he naturally assumed I hadn't either. "Yes! How could you possibly know?" he asked me.

Still not quite believing what I was hearing, I continued, "Did it happen to have an evergreen tree on it?"

Again, Rick was shocked. "How did you know that? I've not shared the dream with anyone!" he exclaimed, pulling an Appeal to Heaven flag from his bag. "I found the flag online and bought you one."

"Too late," I said with a smile, "I already have it."

After giving him a quick explanation, I urged my surprised friend to finish his account of the dream. "Upon reaching the center of the bridge, Dutch, you didn't begin prophesying and decreeing America's destiny, as the others had. Instead, you began waving the flag over the crowd in a figure eight, doing so for about ten minutes. As you did, the people were again passionately worshipping God."

This pattern is important. The number eight on its side—a figure eight—is the symbol of infinity or eternity. In ancient times, when a covenant was ratified by a blood sacrifice, the individuals entering into covenant would actually walk in a figure eight among the pieces of the sacrifice. Why? They were swearing eternal allegiance to the covenant, just as we do in a wedding ceremony with our phrase "'til death do us part." Abraham probably did this when he and God "cut covenant" in Genesis 15.

By waving the evergreen in this "eternal" configuration, I was clearly emphasizing America's covenant with God. "We must honor the power of covenant," I was decreeing with my actions. "If we return to Him, He will war for us, defeating our giants."

Also, by waving this flag, *under which we were born*, I was pointing us back to our roots as a nation—our birth, our purpose and our calling. *The dream is still alive,* the flag was stating. *Go find it. Revisit the stormy seas of the pilgrims, the dusty trails of the pioneers, or the bloody battlefields of Lexington and Concord. Read the sermons of Jonathan Edwards, George Whitefield, or John Wesley until the flame of the First Great Awakening burns in you. Read of Cane*

Ridge, the Second Great Awakening and Charles Finney until you burn with passion to see America become "the shining city on a hill" once again. Tell the old stories! And find the dream.

And, of course, as I waved this ancient flag with its timeless message, I was declaring that we as a nation must once again "appeal to heaven." If we are going to overcome today's giants and recapture our God-given destiny, we must humble ourselves and pray. America had to do this, not only during her fight for freedom, but at many points of her development. When the delegates to the Continental Congress reached an impasse trying to write our Constitution, Ben Franklin made the following appeal.

The small progress we have made after 4 or five weeks close attendance & continual reasonings with each other...is methinks a melancholy proof of the imperfection of the Human Understanding....

...how has it happened, Sir, that we have not hitherto once thought of humbly applying to the Father of lights to illuminate our understandings? In the beginning of the contest with G. Britain, when we were sensible of danger we had daily prayer in this room for the Divine Protection. -- Our prayers, Sir, were heard, and they were graciously answered. All of us who were engaged in the struggle must have observed frequent instances of a Superintending providence in our favor. To that kind providence we owe this happy

opportunity of consulting in peace on the means of establishing our future national felicity. And have we now forgotten that powerful friend?

I have lived, Sir, a long time and the longer I live, the more convincing proofs I see of this truth -- that God governs in the affairs of men. And if a sparrow cannot fall to the ground without his notice, is it probable that an empire can rise without his aid? We have been assured, Sir, in the sacred writings that "except the Lord build they labor in vain that build it." I firmly believe this; and I also believe that without his concurring aid we shall succeed in this political building no better than the Builders of Babel: We shall be divided by our little partial local interests; our projects will be confounded, and we ourselves shall be become a reproach and a bye word down to future age.

I therefore beg leave to move -- that henceforth prayers imploring the assistance of Heaven, and its blessings on our deliberations, be held in this Assembly every morning before we proceed to business, and that one or more of the Clergy of this City be requested to officiate in that service.[1]

If our government leaders today would humble themselves and appeal to heaven for wisdom, we would experience the same divine assistance the framers found. Many, thank God, are beginning to do so. Let's join them, asking God for His intervention in our land.

The Harvest Of The Ages

Rick then finished his account of the dream with one last, powerful statement. "After several minutes, you stopped waving the flag and began prophesying over America, just as the previous six representatives had done." He couldn't recall what I had said, except for the last sentence, which I'm certain was all he was intended to remember. With great conviction and authority, I declared, "America is returning to the ancient path, in order to reap the harvest of the ages!"

End of dream.

To say I was impacted by this dream would be the understatement of the year. Its message touched a deep place in my soul, confirming what I have believed for many years: the greatest harvest of all time is ahead of us. It is now in the birth canal, ready for the final push. And America, though we may not look like it at the moment, has an important part to play in this great harvest. The Lord still has need of us.

Get ready!

Rally to the flag. God has resurrected it for such a time as this. Wave it outwardly; wear it inwardly. Appeal to heaven daily for a spiritual revolution that will knock out the Goliaths of our day.

Put yourself in the storyline, because the stories are your stories. Let your heart revive as you think about the great God of yesterday, today and forever, You're on His team, part of His plan. You're in the dream.

Get dressed and step into the ring. Wear both gloves—Everlast and Evergreen. Be assured they are powerful, secret weapons, filled with heaven's knock-out ability. We're in covenant with the Everlasting God. Throw His weight around! Declare His favor and blessing over America. By faith, call her back to the ancient path, to reap the harvest of the ages. Believe He can; believe He will.

Are you ready to take your place in the synergy of the ages?

ENDNOTES

Introduction
[1] Adams, John. "Argument in Defense of the British Soldiers in the Boston Massacre Trials." December 4, 1770.
[2] Franklin, Benjamin. "Constitutional Convention Address on Prayer." June 28, 1787. Philadelphia, PA.

Chapter 1
[1] Quoted in Leonard Ravenhill, "Jonathan Edwards: Portrait of a Revival Preacher," *Dayspring,* 1963. www.ravenhill.org/edwards.htm.

Chapter 4
[1] Everlast Worldwide, Inc. "About Everlast." 2015. http://www.everlast.com/about
[2] Lincoln, Abraham. "Proclamation: Appointing a Day of National Humiliation, Fasting, and Prayer." March 30, 1863.

Chapter 5
[1] Locke, John. *The Second Treatise of Civil Government.* "Chapter XIV, Of Prerogative, Section 168." 1690.

[2] Winthrop, John. "A Model of Christian Charity." 1630.

[3] The Mayflower Compact. 1620.

[4] Kennedy, John F. "The City Upon A Hill." Speech Given at Massachusetts General Court. January 9, 1961.

Reagan, Ronald. "We will Be a City Upon A Hill." Speech Given at the First Conservative Political Action Conference. January 25, 1974.

Also quoted by Presidents John Adams, Alexander Hamilton, George Washington, James Madison, Abraham Lincoln, Ulysses S. Grant, Woodrow Wilson, Calvin Coolidge, Franklin D. Roosevelt, and Bill Clinton.

[5] American Memory. "Col. Joseph Reed to Col. John Glover and Stephen Moylan." October 20 1775. *The Library of Congress.* Memmory.loc.gov/mssp/mgw/mgw3b/001/08504.jpg

[6] Naval History and Heritage Command. "The U.S. Navy's First Jack." *U.S. Navy.* Published December 17, 2014. www.history.navy.mil/browse-by-topic/heritage/banners/usnavy-first-jack.html

[7] Prepared by Gerald Murphy (The Cleveland Free-Net-aa300). "The Great Law of Peace, Gayanashagowa." The Constitution of the Iroquois Nations. Distributed by the Cybercasting Services Division of the National Telecomputing Network (NTPN). www.iroquoisdemocracy.pdx.edu/hteml/greatlaw.html
Section 1: *"I am Dekanawidah and with the Five Nations' Confederate Lords I plant the Tree of Great Peace. I plant it in your territory, Adodarhoh, and the Onondaga Nation, in the territory of you who are Firekeepers. I name the tree the Tree of the Great Long Leaves..."*
Section 65: *"I, Dekanawida, and the Union Lords, now uproot the tallest pine tree and into the cavity thereby made we cast all weapons of war. Into the depths of the earth, down into the deep underearth currents of water flowing to unknown regions we cast all the weapons of strife. We bury them from sight and we plant again the tree. Thus shall the Great Peace be established and hostilities shall no longer be known between the Five Nations but peace to the United People."*

[8] Franklin, Benjamin. Letter to James Parker on the Iroquois League. 1751.
www.smithsoniansource.org/display/primarysource/vie wdetails.aspx?PrimarySourceld=1198

Feathers, Cynthia and Feathers, Susan. "Franklin and the Iroquois Foundations of the Constitution." The Pennsylvania Gazette. January 5, 2007.
http://www.upenn.edu/gazette/0107/gaz09.html

[9] U.S. Department of State: Office of the Historian. "Albany Plan of the Union, 1754."
https://history.state.gov/milestones/1750-1775/albany-plan

[10] United States Senate. "H. Con. Res. 331." 100th Congress, 2nd Session. October 5, 1988.
http://www.senate.gov/reference/resources/pdf/hconres 331.pdf

[11] The Declaration of Independence. July 4, 1776.

Chapter 6

[1] Franklin, Benjamin. "Constitutional Convention Address on Prayer." June 28, 1787. Philadelphia, PA.

About The Author

Dutch Sheets is an internationally recognized teacher, conference speaker, and best-selling author. He has written over twenty books, many of which have been translated into more than thirty languages. His international bestseller, *Intercessory Prayer*, has sold over a million copies worldwide and is being used to empower believers for passionate prayer and societal transformation.

Seeing America experience a sweeping revival and return to its Godly heritage is Dutch's greatest passion. He is a messenger of hope for America, encouraging believers to contend for awakening in our day and reformation in our lifetime.

Dutch and Ceci, his wife of over 37 years, love the mountains and spending time with their family and grandchildren.

To learn more, visit www.dutchsheets.org.

Also Available From Dutch Sheets

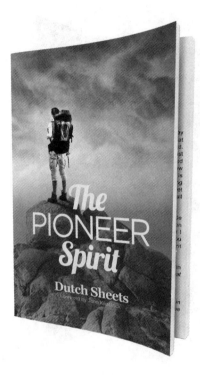

Do you seem to walk to the beat of a different drum? Don't fit the mold? Can't stand religiosity or compromise? God has set you apart as a forerunner for His Kingdom! The Pioneer Spirit is your open door to the exciting, trailblazing journey God destined for your life.

www.dutchsheets.org

Also Available From Dutch Sheets

In honor of his memory, Dutch published this collection of his father's writings, paired with select portions from Dutch's books. If you'd like a condensed version of the wisdom that helped shape Dutch's life and ministry, you'll find this 90-day devotional to be a treasure!

www.dutchsheets.org

Dutch Sheets Ministries
Monthly Partnership Program

We invite you to join us in carrying the Appeal to Heaven message across this great nation.

With each monthly donation of $25 or more you will receive:

Dutch Sheets' latest teaching
A letter from Dutch
Valuable gifts and resources
Special discounts to our store

Partner with us to bring awakening and revival to America. Together, we can do it again!

To learn more about our
Ministry Partnership Program
visit: www.dutchsheets.org.

TEACH | AWAKEN | REFORM

NOTES

NOTES

NOTES

NOTES

NOTES